touch

First U.S. edition published 1985 by Barron's Educational Series, Inc.

All inquiries should be addressed to:
Barron's Educational Series, Inc.
250 Wireless Boulevard
Hauppauge, New York 11788

International Standard Book No. 0-8120-3567-4

Library of Congress Catalog Card No. 84-28210

Library of Congress Cataloging in Publication Data

Parramón, José María
  The fives senses—touch.

  Translation of: Los cinco sentidos—el tacto.
  Summary: A short scientific explanation of our sense
of touch.
  1. Touch—Juvenile literature. [1. Touch.   2. Senses
and sensation]   I. Puig, J.J.   II. Rius, María, ill.
III. Title.
QP451.P3613   1985   612'.88   84-29766
ISBN 0-8120-3567-4

Printed in Spain

26 25 24 23 22 21 20 19 18

the five senses

touch

María Rius

J.M. Parramón   J.J. Puig

BARRON'S

When you touch a rose petal it feels soft… very, very soft!

But the thorns are sharp… very, very sharp!

Feel how smooth the ice is.

Feel the rough bark.

The sand is very dry.

The water is very wet!

Fire is very, very hot!

Snow is very, very cold!

The mirror feels hard.

The mattress feels soft.

But the softest, best thing of all to touch is a fluffy little lamb.

The way you know how something feels is by touching it with your SKIN.

TOUCH

Your *skin* covers you all over. Not only does your skin protect you, but it is also your largest sense organ. When you touch something, your skin can tell you whether it is hot or cold, rough or smooth, wet or dry, hard or soft. It can also tell you any combination of those feelings. Your skin can tell you that something is hot, and wet, and rough—all at once!

There are *nerve endings* just below the *epidermis,* or surface of your skin, all over your body. These nerve endings carry messages to your brain all the time, telling you what kind of thing you are touching. Your brain then figures out what to do about it. For example, if you touch a hot pot, the nerve endings in your skin send a message back to your brain that says: *Hot!* Your brain then sends a message back to your finger: *Move!* And you do it, right?

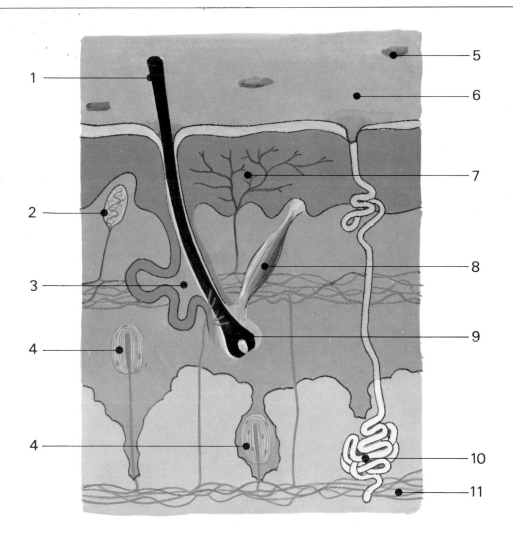

THE SKIN

1 Hair shaft
2 Meissner's corpuscles
3 Sebaceous glands
4 Pacinian corpuscles
5 Pores
6 Epidermis
7 Nerve endings
8 Muscle
9 Hair follicle
10 Sweat gland
11 Blood vessels

TOUCH

This is how your sense of touch works. Your skin is the most interesting of all your five senses. It's really five senses all rolled up into one. Not only can you feel with your skin, but you can "see" with your skin, too. How many times have you felt the shape of something when your eyes were closed—and been able to guess what it was? Blind people can almost "see" what objects are by touching them. Blind people learn to use their fingertips instead of their eyes for reading. There is a special alphabet made of little bumps on the paper. By running your fingers across the bumps, you can read. This special alphabet is called Braille.

You can also "hear" with your skin. Put your fingers lightly on the speaker of your record player. You can feel the vibrations made by the music. Deaf people are sometimes taught to "hear" people speak by holding their fingertips against the throat of the person speaking. They can feel the sound vibrations this way, and it helps them figure out what the person is saying.

Of course, you can't smell or taste things with your skin...not really. But remember, your skin covers you all over. It lines the inside of your nose, which does your smelling, and it covers your tongue, which does your tasting.

Your sense of touch does double work. When you touch something, you not only feel what it feels like, but you can also sense that you are being touched by something as well. When you press hard on something, you also feel the pressure of the thing against your skin. If you press too hard, it may hurt you. There are special nerve endings for feeling pressure. These are called *Pacinian corpuscles.*

The skin senses work together as teams. There are hot and cold, wet and dry, rough and smooth, hard and soft. Every part of your skin has nerves to feel all these different feelings. There are more nerve endings in the tips of your fingers than practically anywhere else, which is why it hurts so much when you get a tiny cut on your finger. There are also nerve endings that are found particularly in the palms of your hands and soles of your feet, called *Meissner's corpuscles.*

Sending your brain pain messages is one of the important jobs of your skin. It's your body's way of telling you to "cut that out!" You would probably like it better if things didn't hurt at all, but pain helps you take good care of your body. Your skin also protects you from germs. It is like having a large, head-to-foot-size Band-Aid that keeps out dirt and germs.

Your hair is also part of your skin. Your hair protects you from the sun and can tell you which way the wind is blowing, too.

Your skin is one of your most important senses, so take good care of it—it tells you all sorts of things, doesn't it?